THE TWENTY-SIX RUDIMENTS OF DRUMMING

... and How to Play Them

Daily practice of the Twenty-Six Rudiments of Drumming is one of the most important mediums whereby ambitious players can quickly and thoroughly acquire a high degree of technical proficiency on the snare drum. The rudiments upon which the technique of snare drum playing rests, correspond to the scales upon which the technique of playing wind and string instruments is dependent. Too much stress cannot be placed upon the mastery of these rudiments, for without such a mastery, a performer on the drums is seriously handicapped, particularly when playing drums in a legitimate fashion.

Ability to execute the first thirteen of these rudiments is a requirement for membership in the *National Association of Rudimental Drummers,* but the serious student of drums should not restrict himself to these basic rudiments; rather, he should become acquainted with all twenty-six of the rudiments, and become the master of them all. Rudiment No. 25, commonly referred to as "Lesson No. 25," was given a new name some years ago by the eminent drum authority, *Mr. William F. Ludwig,* when he referred to it as the "Ratatap." This new appellation, given to an old rudiment, has been adhered to in the present work.

In preparing *Reviewing the Rudiments,* the thought paramount in the writer's mind has been that of presenting the various snare drum rudiments in an up-to-date, modern setting, thoroughly purposeful throughout, and fashioned to sustain student interest from beginning to end. To facilitate teaching procedures when using the present volume in ensemble classes, a system of consecutive numbering of the many studies has been followed throughout, while rehearsal marks have been placed also in all of the various exercises and etudes.

Ambitious students who take advantage of the valuable study material contained within the pages of the present volume will find themselves well repaid for the time spent in practicing the contents of the book. Increased technical proficiency, making it possible for the achievement of higher musical standards, backed by the self assurance that comes to performers well equipped for surmounting any difficulties they might encounter in playing the drum parts of advanced musical compositions, is in itself worthy justification for all efforts directed along the channels of rudimental drum practice.

Harvey S. Whistler

7777 W. BLUEMOUND RD. P.O. BOX 13819 MILWAUKEE, WI 53213

T0050632

The Twenty Six Rudiments of Drumming

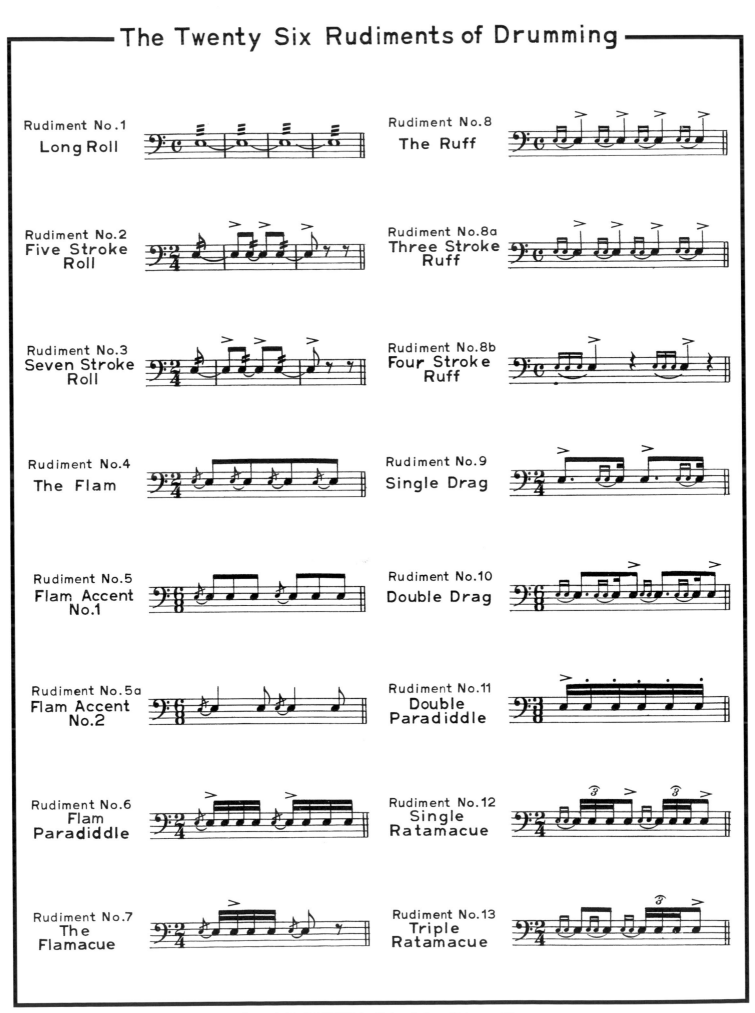

Copyright Renewed
Copyright MCMXLVI by Rubank, Inc., Chicago, Ill.
International Copyright Secured

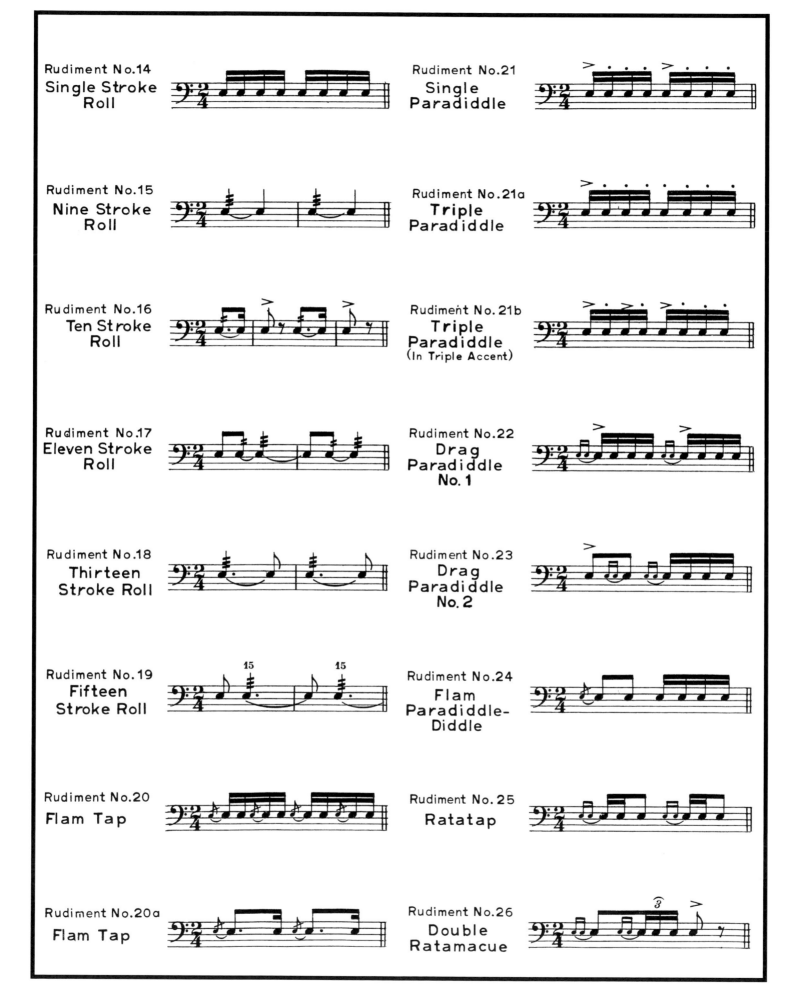

Rudiment No.1: The Long Roll

Repeat each exercise many times; gradually increase the tempo until the desired effect is obtained.

Developing the Rudiment

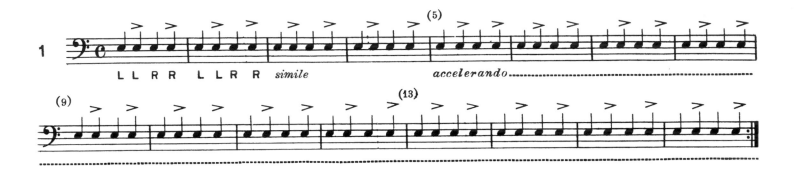

Basic Exercise

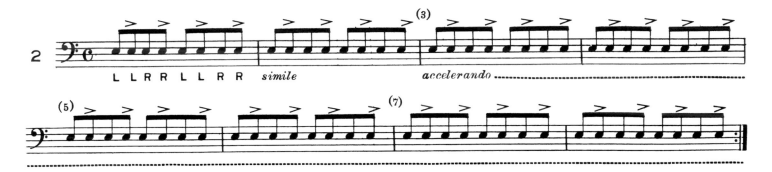

Technic Builder

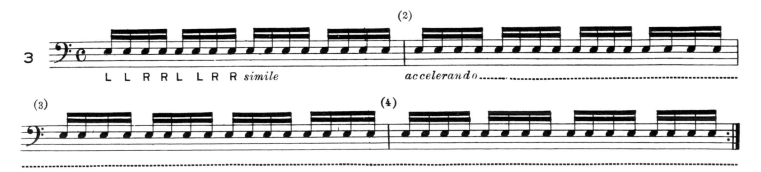

The Long Roll

Rudiment No.2: The Five Stroke Roll

Developing the Rudiment

Rudiment No.3: The Seven Stroke Roll

Developing the Rudiment

Basic Exercise

Technic Builder

The Seven Stroke Roll

Rudiment No.4: The Flam

Right Hand Flam

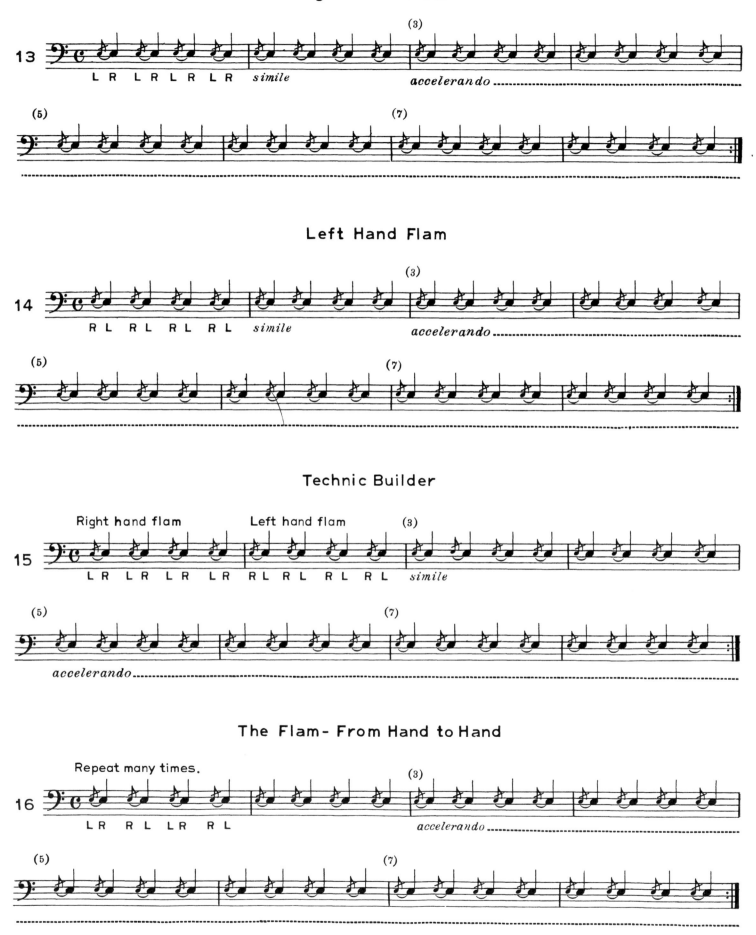

Left Hand Flam

Technic Builder

The Flam - From Hand to Hand

Rudiment No. 5: The Flam Accent No. 1

Developing the Rudiment

Flam Accent No. 1 in $\frac{3}{8}$ Time (Meter)

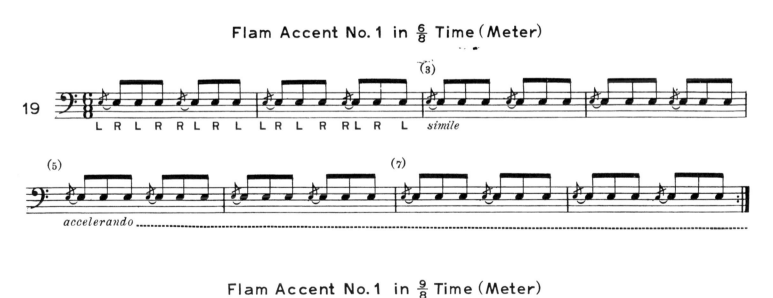

Flam Accent No. 1 in $\frac{6}{8}$ Time (Meter)

Flam Accent No. 1 in $\frac{9}{8}$ Time (Meter)

Rudiment No.5a: The Flam Accent No.2

Developing the Rudiment

Rudiment No.6: The Flam Paradiddle

Developing the Rudiment

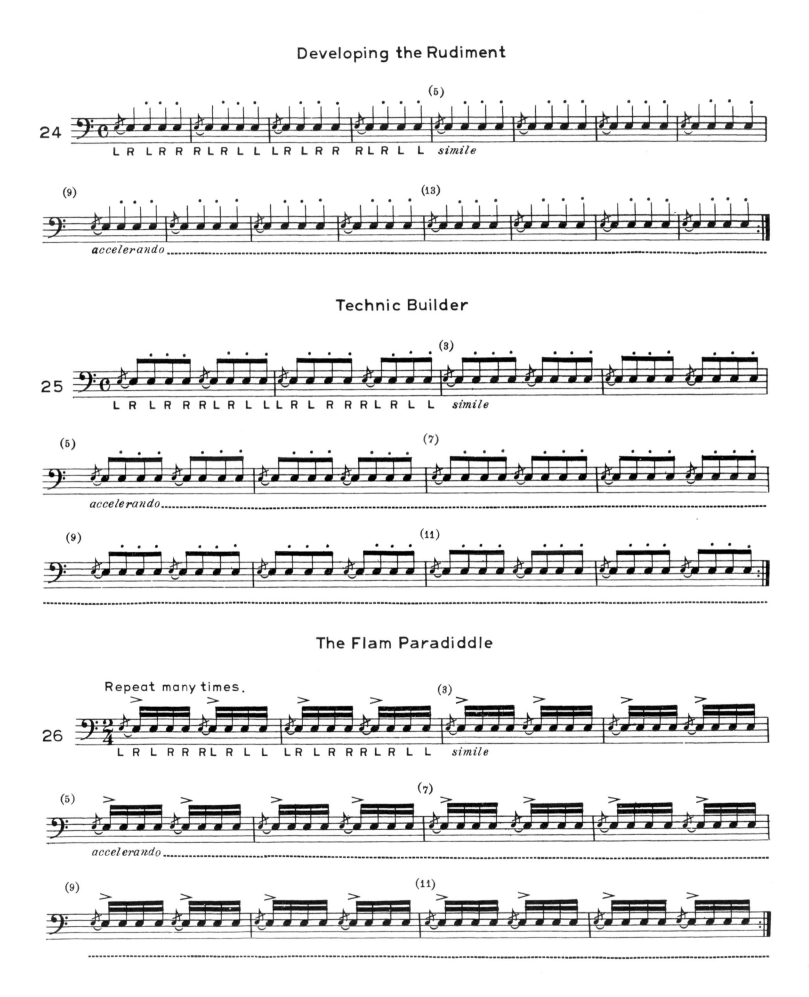

Technic Builder

The Flam Paradiddle

Rudiment No.7: The Flamacue

Developing the Rudiment

Technic Builder

The Flamacue

Repeat many times.

Rudiment No.8: The Ruff

Developing the Rudiment

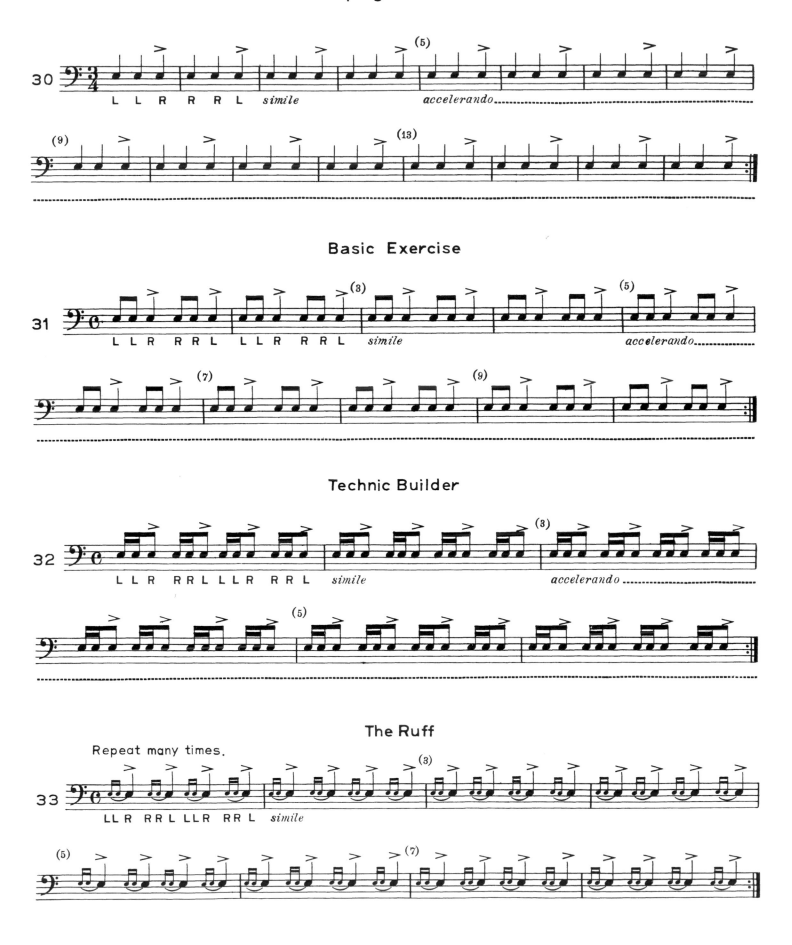

Basic Exercise

Technic Builder

The Ruff

Rudiment No. 8a: The Three Stroke Ruff

Rudiment No. 8b: The Four Stroke Ruff

Developing the Four Stroke Ruff

The Four Stroke Ruff

Rudiment No.9: The Single Drag

Developing the Rudiment

Basic Exercise

Technic Builder

The Single Drag

Rudiment No.10: The Double Drag

Developing the Rudiment

Basic Exercise

Technic Builder

The Double Drag

Repeat many times.

Rudiment No.11: The Double Paradiddle

Developing the Rudiment

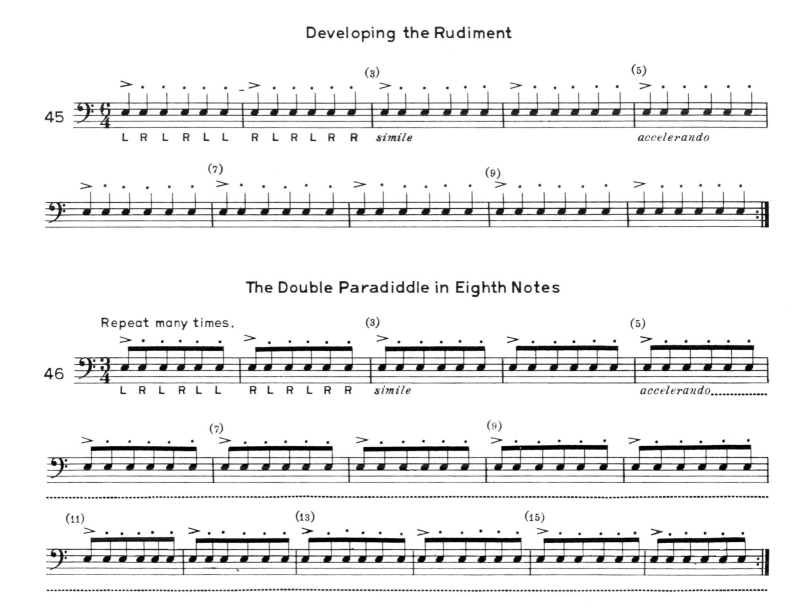

The Double Paradiddle in Eighth Notes

The Double Paradiddle in Sixteenth Notes

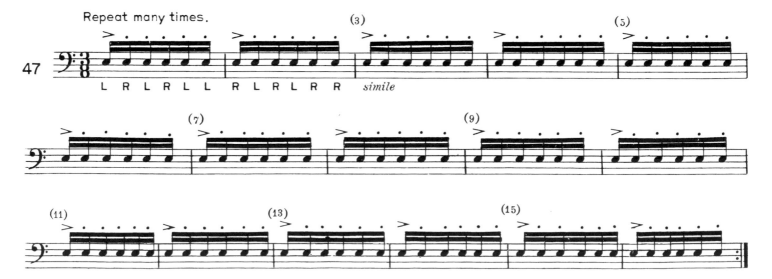

Rudiment No.12: The Single Ratamacue

Developing the Rudiment

Basic Exercise

Technic Builder

The Single Ratamacue

Rudiment No. 13: The Triple Ratamacue

Developing the Rudiment

Basic Exercise

Technic Builder

The Triple Ratamacue

Rudiment No.14: The Single Stroke Roll

Developing the Rudiment

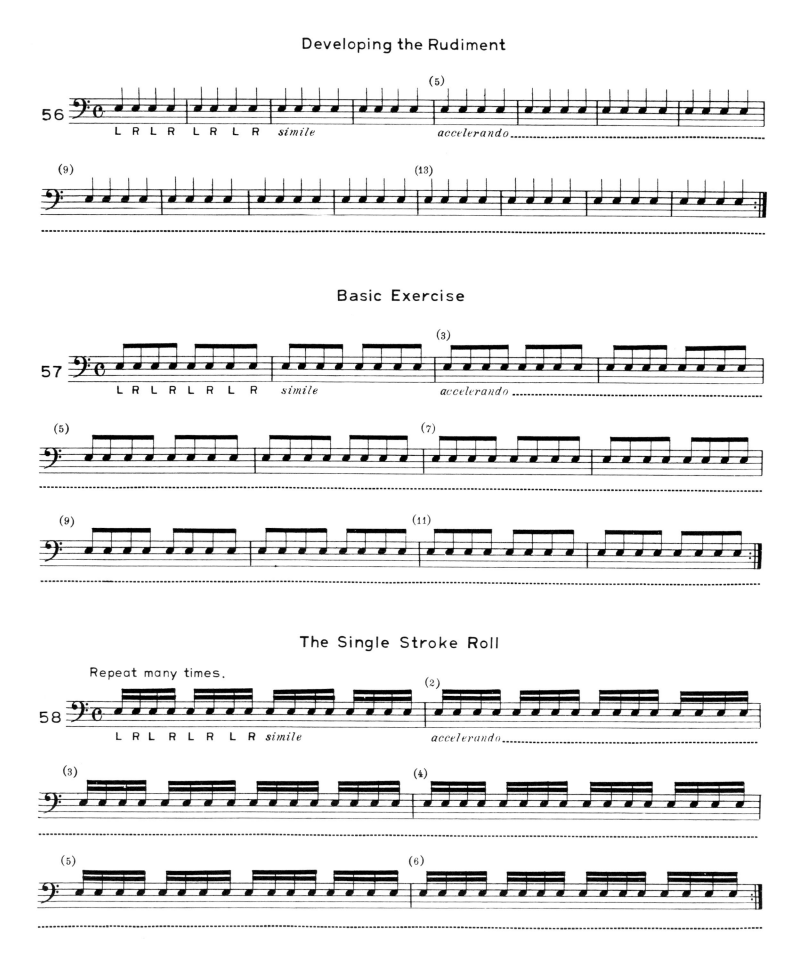

Basic Exercise

The Single Stroke Roll

Rudiment No.15: The Nine Stroke Roll

Developing the Rudiment

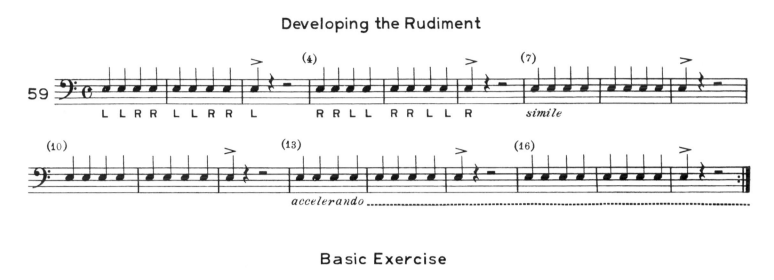

Basic Exercise

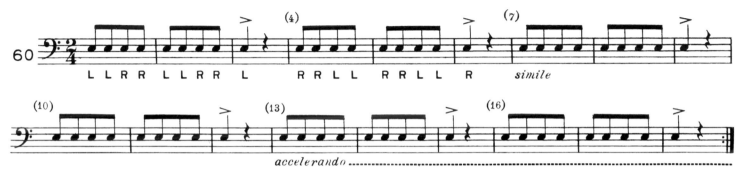

Technic Builder

The Nine Stroke Roll

Rudiment No.16: The Ten Stroke Roll

Developing the Rudiment

Rudiment No.17: The Eleven Stroke Roll

Developing the Rudiment

67

L L R R   L L R   R L L R   *simile*   *accelerando*................

(10)   (13)   (16)

Basic Exercise

68

L L R R   L L R R   L L R   *simile*   *accelerando*................

(10)   (13)   (16)

Technic Builder

69

L L R R L L R R   L L R   *simile*   *accelerando*................

(7)   (9)   (11)

The Eleven Stroke Roll

Repeat many times.

70

L L R R   L L R R   L L R

(9)   (13)

Rudiment No.18: The Thirteen Stroke Roll

Developing the Rudiment

71

L L R R L L R R L L R R L   R R L L R R L L R R L L R

(9)   (13)

simile
accelerando

Basic Exercise

72

L L R R L L R R L L R R L   R R L L R R L L R R L L R

(9)   (13)

simile
accelerando

Technic Builder

73

L L R R L L R R L L R R L   R R L L R R L L R R L L R

(5)   (7)

simile
accelerando

The Thirteen Stroke Roll

Repeat many times.   (5)

74

L L R R L L R R L L R R L
R R L L R R L L R R L L R

(9)   (13)

Rudiment No.19: The Fifteen Stroke Roll

Developing the Rudiment

Basic Exercise

Technic Builder

The Fifteen Stroke Roll

Rudiment No.20: The Flam Tap

Developing the Rudiment

The Flam Tap in Eighth Notes

The Flam Tap in Sixteenth Notes

The Flam on a Dotted Eighth Note Followed by a Sixteenth Note Tap

Rudiment No. 21: The Single Paradiddle

Developing the Rudiment

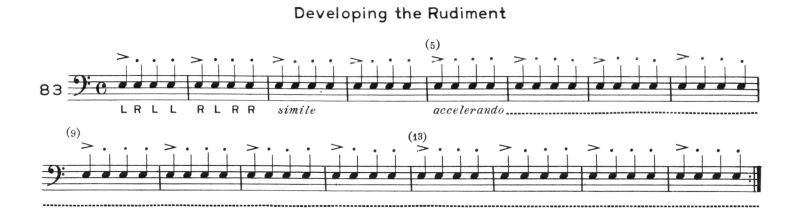

Basic Exercise

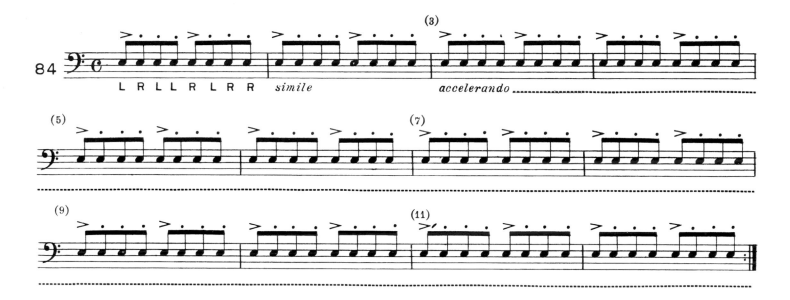

The Single Paradiddle

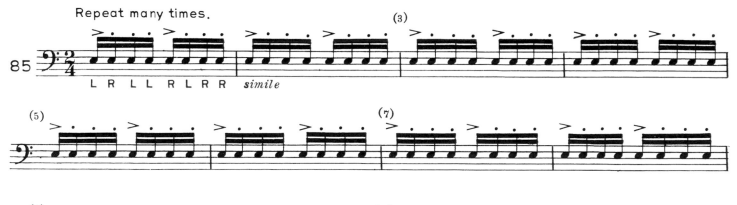

Rudiment No. 21a: The Triple Paradiddle

(A Compound Rudiment)

Developing the Rudiment

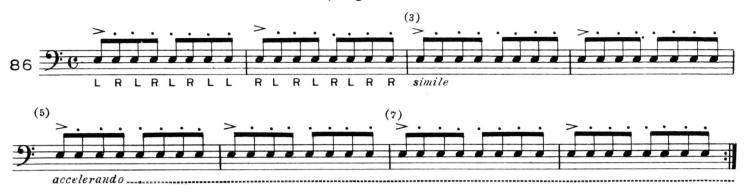

The Triple Paradiddle

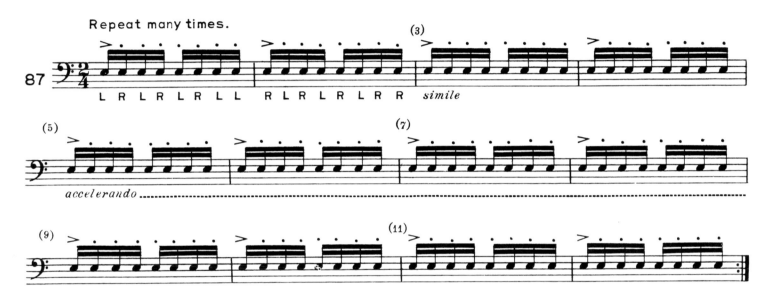

The Triple Paradiddle in Triple Accent

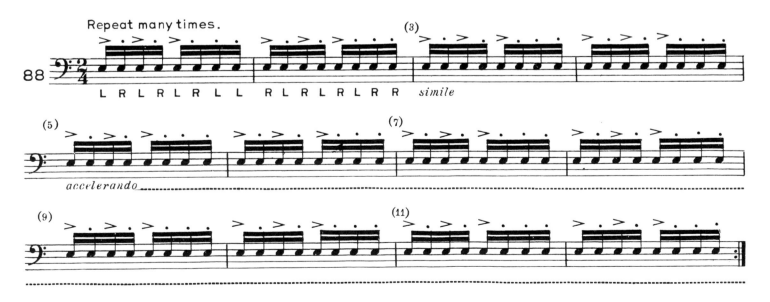

Rudiment No. 22: The Drag Paradiddle No.1

Developing the Rudiment

Technic Builder

The Drag Paradiddle No.1

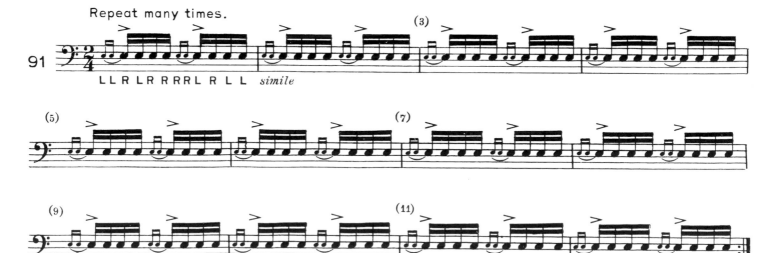

Rudiment No.23: The Drag Paradiddle No.2

Developing the Rudiment

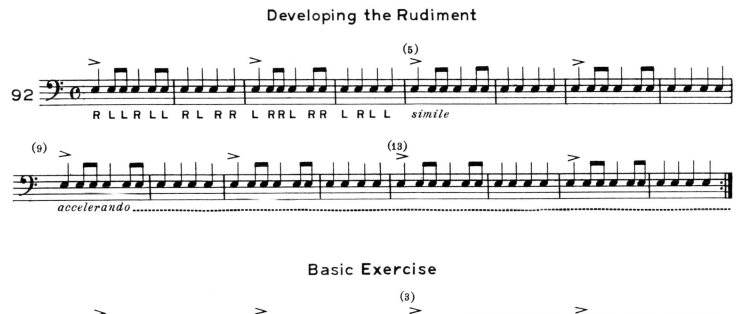

R L L R L L R L R R   L R R L R R   L R L L   *simile*

accelerando

Basic Exercise

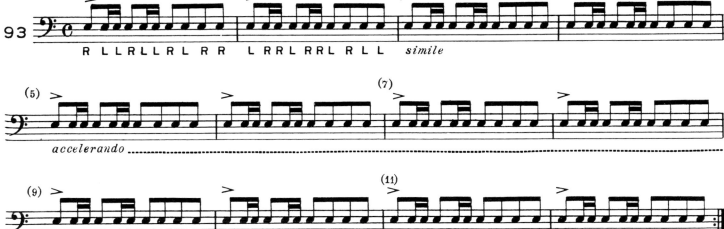

R L L R L L R L R R   L R R L R R L R L L   *simile*

accelerando

The Drag Paradiddle No.2

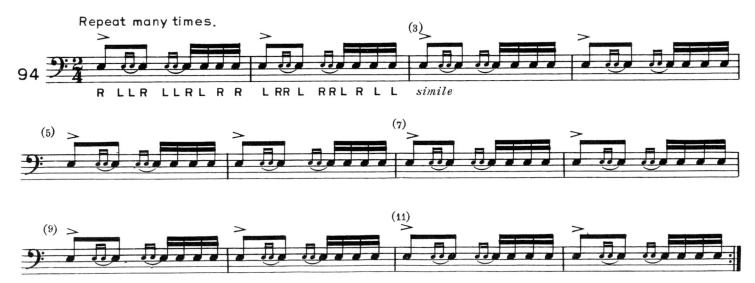

Repeat many times.

R L L R L L R L R R   L R R L R R L R L L   *simile*

Rudiment No. 24: The Flam Paradiddle-Diddle

Developing the Rudiment

Basic Exercise

The Flam Paradiddle-Diddle

Rudiment No. 25: The Ratatap

Commonly known as "Lesson No.25", this rudiment has been designated "The Ratatap" by the eminent drum authority, William F. Ludwig.

Developing the Rudiment

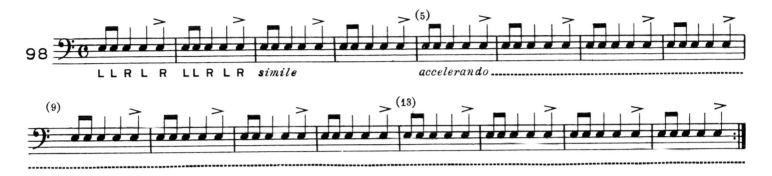

The Ratatap

The Ratatap - After the Beat

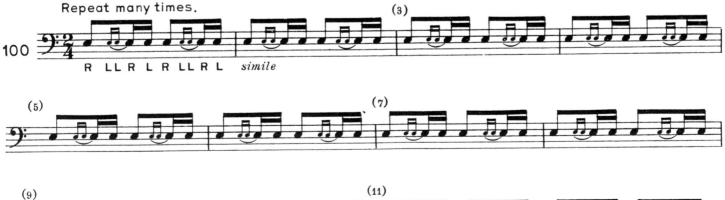

Rudiment No. 26: The Double Ratamacue

Developing the Rudiment

The Double Ratamacue in $\frac{3}{4}$ Time (Meter)

The Double Ratamacue in $\frac{2}{4}$ Time (Meter)

Drum Etudes

Based on the Rudiments of Drumming

Long Roll Etude
(Rudiment No.1)

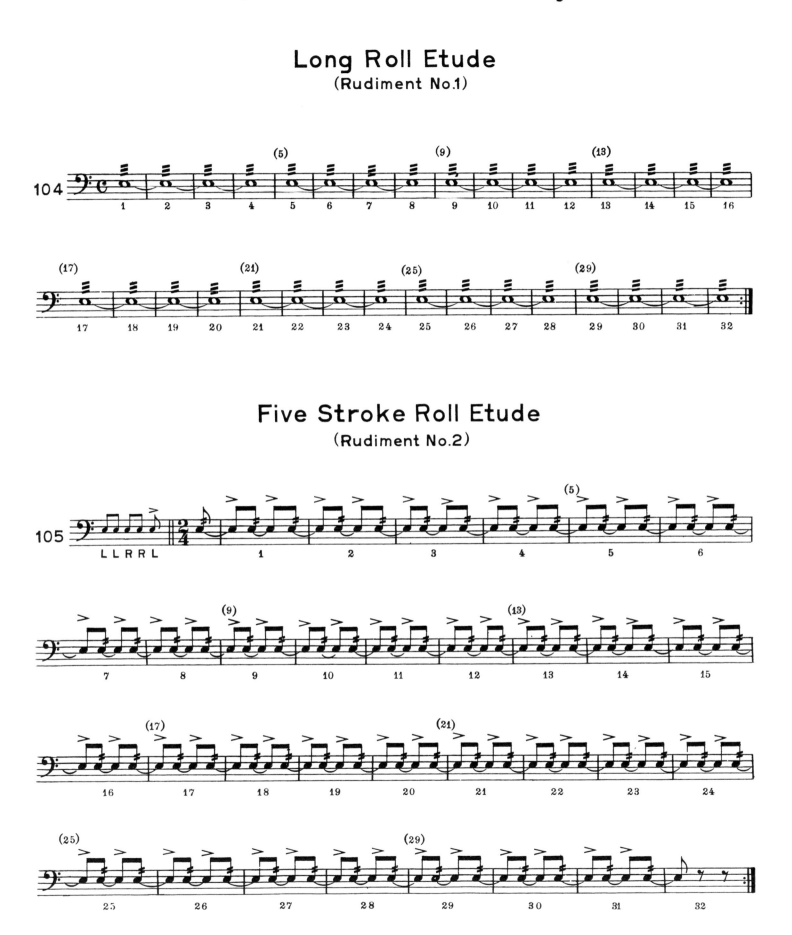

Five Stroke Roll Etude
(Rudiment No.2)

Seven Stroke Roll Etude
(Rudiment No.3)

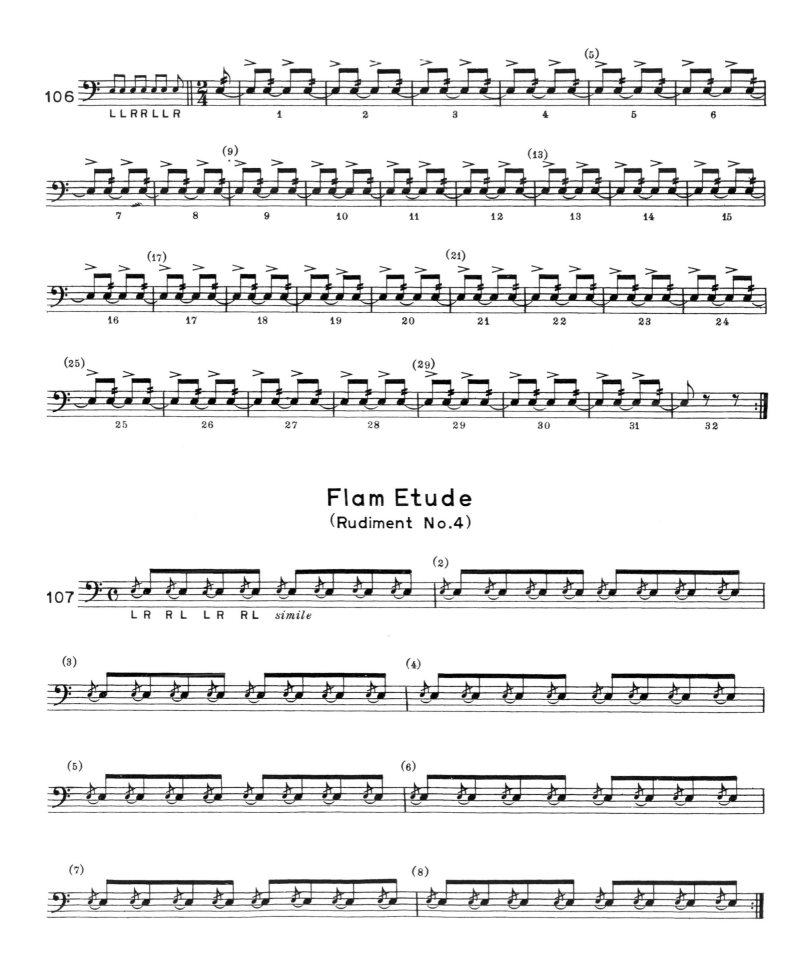

Flam Etude
(Rudiment No.4)

Flam Accent No.1 Etude
(Rudiment No.5)

Flam Accent No.2 Etude
(Rudiment No.5a)

Flam Paradiddle Etude
(Rudiment No.6)

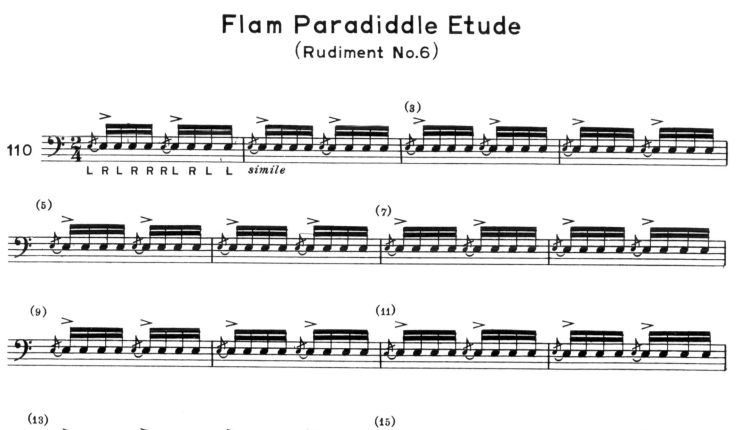

110

L R L R R R L R L L *simile*

(3)

(5) (7)

(9) (11)

(13) (15)

Flamacue Etude
(Rudiment No.7)

111

L R L R L L R *simile*

(3)

(5) (7)

(9) (11)

(13) (15)

Ruff Etude
(Rudiment No.8)

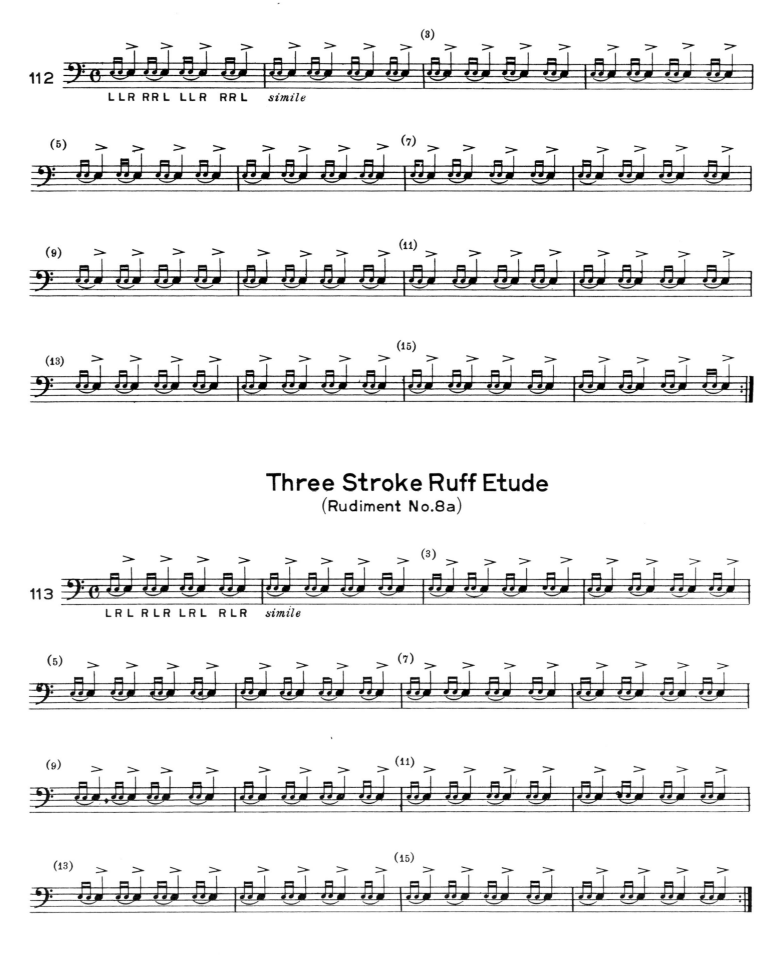

Three Stroke Ruff Etude
(Rudiment No.8a)

Four Stroke Ruff Etude
(Rudiment No.8b)

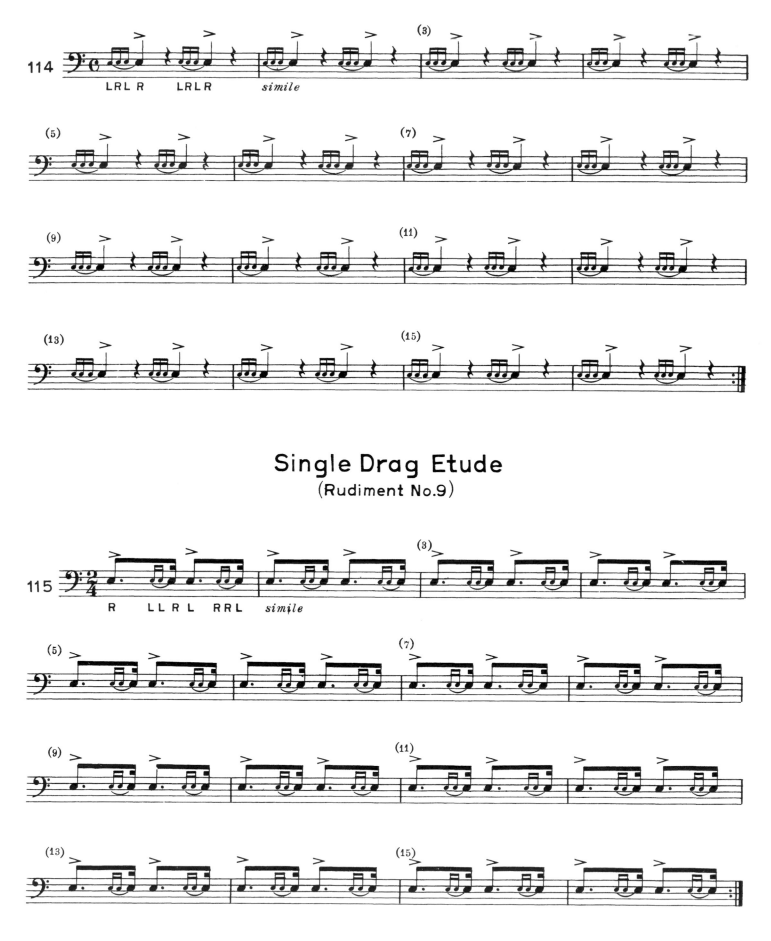

Single Drag Etude
(Rudiment No.9)

Double Drag Etude
(Rudiment No.10)

Double Paradiddle Etude
(Rudiment No.11)

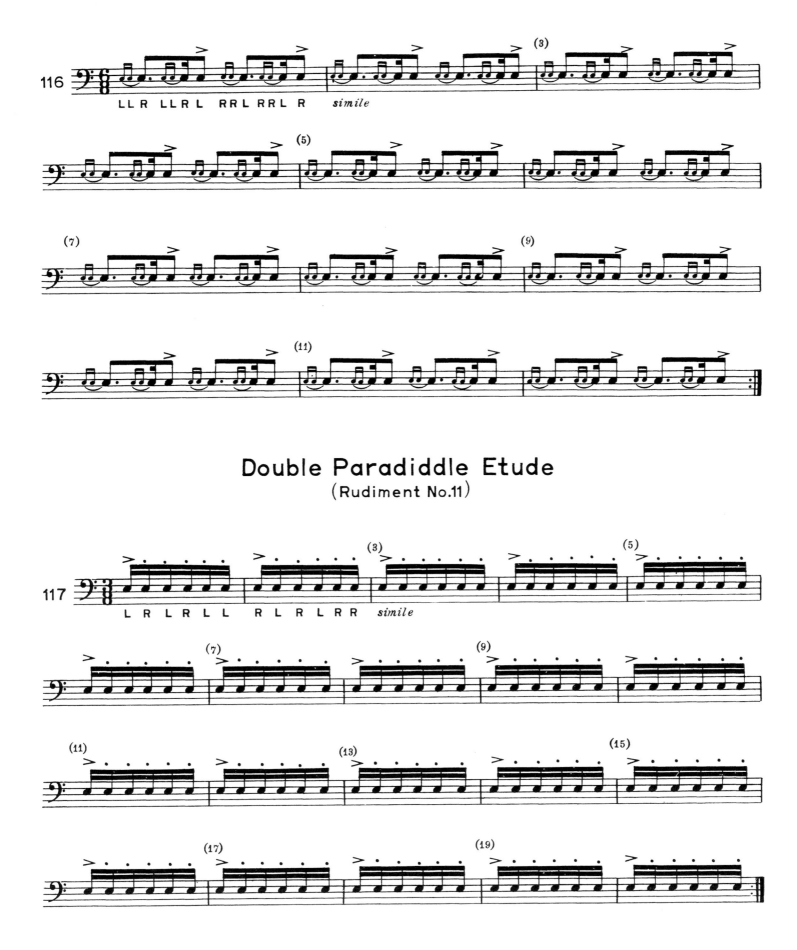

Single Ratamacue Etude
(Rudiment No.12)

Triple Ratamacue Etude
(Rudiment No.13)

Single Stroke Roll Etude
(Rudiment No.14)

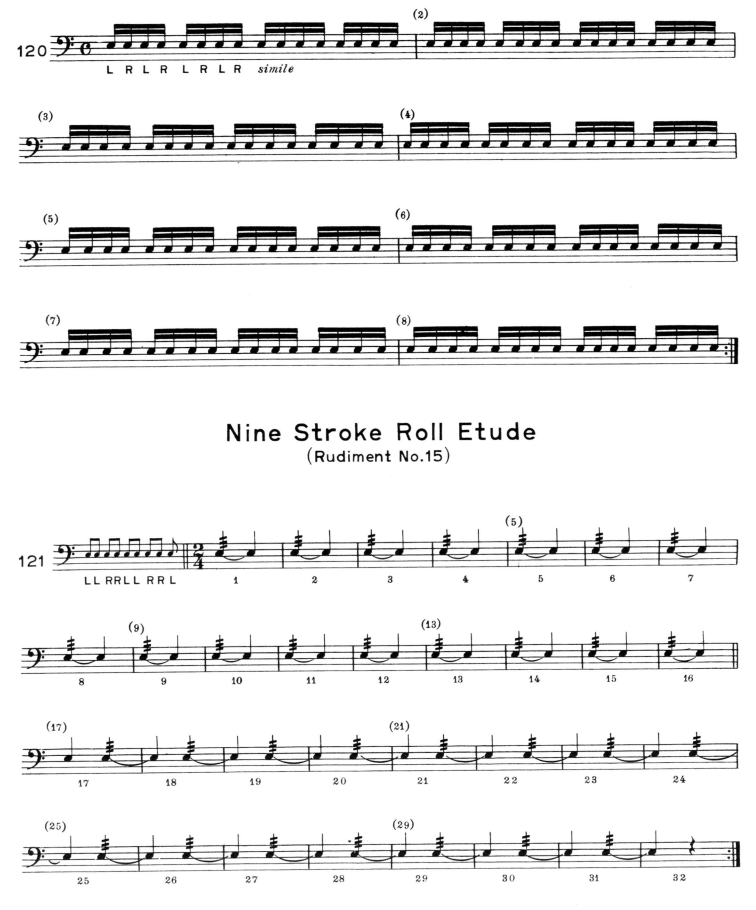

Nine Stroke Roll Etude
(Rudiment No.15)

Ten Stroke Roll Etude
(Rudiment No.16)

Eleven Stroke Roll Etude
(Rudiment No.17)

Thirteen Stroke Roll Etude
(Rudiment No.18)

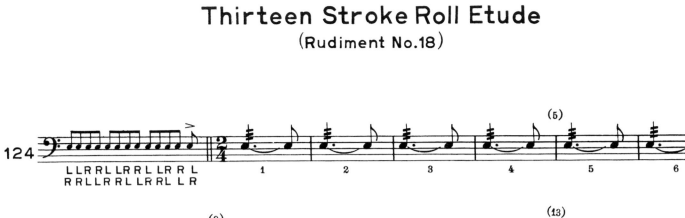

Fifteen Stroke Roll Etude
(Rudiment No.19)

Flam Tap Etude
(Rudiment No.20)

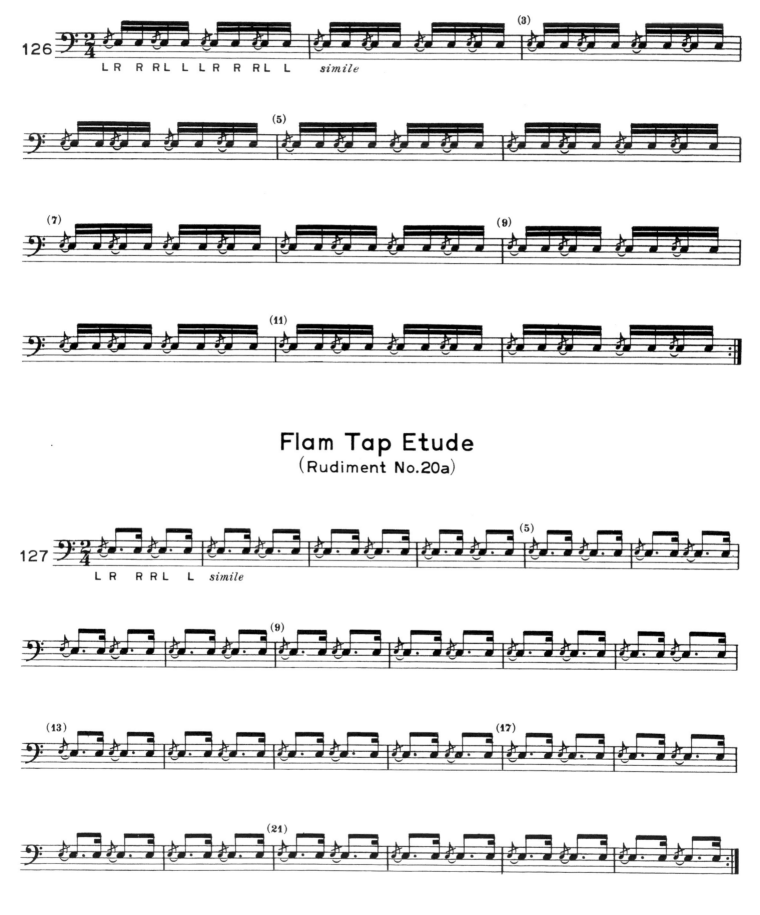

Flam Tap Etude
(Rudiment No.20a)

Single Paradiddle Etude
(Rudiment No.21)

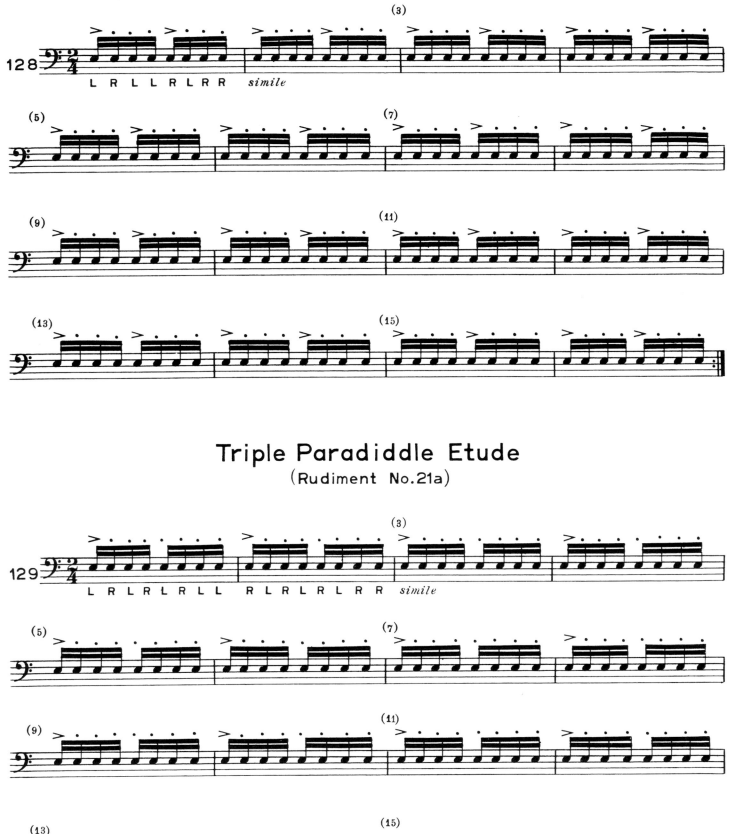

Triple Paradiddle Etude
(Rudiment No.21a)

Triple Paradiddle Etude (In Triple Accent)
(Rudiment No.21b)

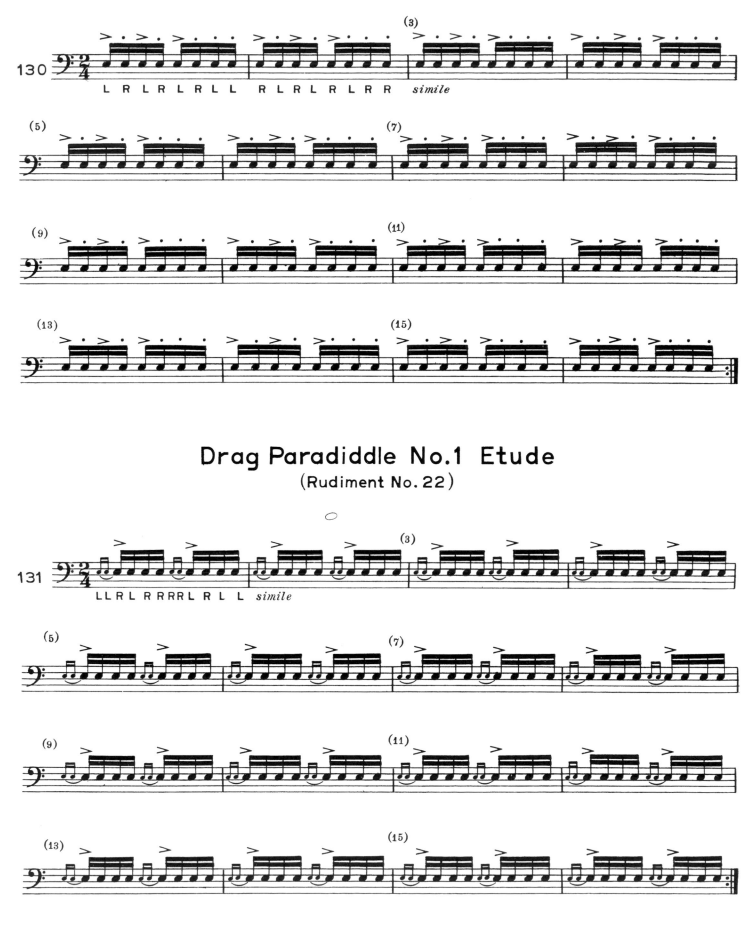

Drag Paradiddle No.1 Etude
(Rudiment No. 22)

Drag Paradiddle No.2 Etude
(Rudiment No.23)

Flam Paradiddle-Diddle Etude
(Rudiment No.24)

Ratatap Etude
(Rudiment No.25)

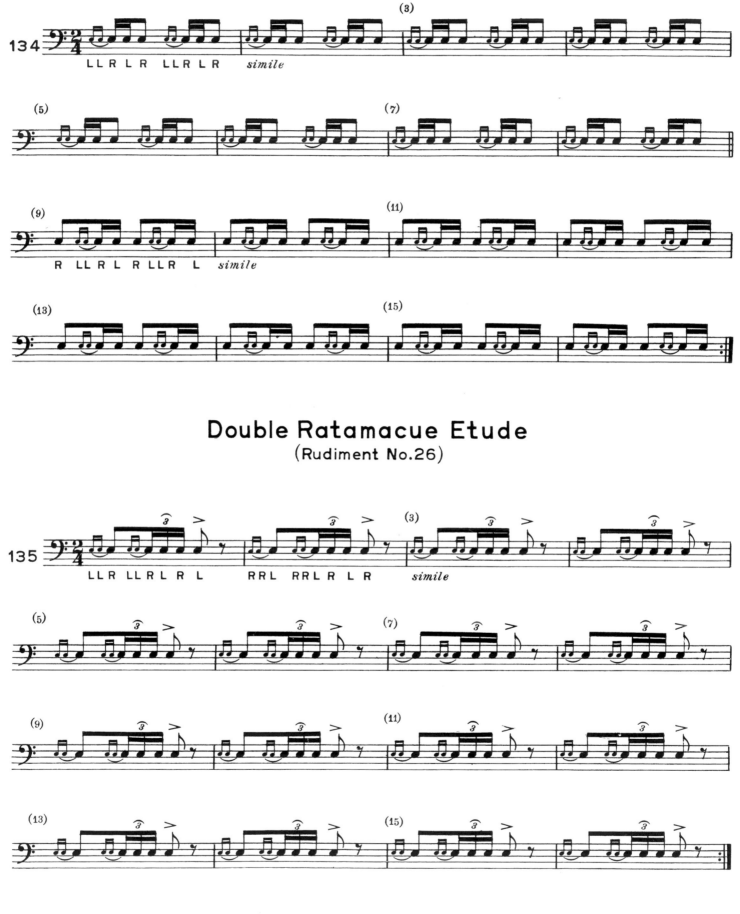

Double Ratamacue Etude
(Rudiment No.26)